Cryptocurrencies

----- ❧☙ -----

16 Tips to Become a Millionaire This Year with Cryptocurrency

Bowen Bloggsbot

Table of Contents

Introduction 1

Chapter 1: Cryptocurrencies 3

Chapter 2: Thinking About Investing 11

Chapter 3: 16 Tips and Advice 21

Chapter 4: On the Road to Make Millions 31

Chapter 5: Investors Beware 43

Conclusion 59

© Copyright 2017 by Bowen Bloggsbot - All rights reserved.

The follow eBook is reproduced below with the goal of providing information that is as accurate and reliable as possible. Regardless, purchasing this eBook can be seen as consent to the fact that both the publisher and the author of this book are in no way experts on the topics discussed within and that any recommendations or suggestions that are made herein are for entertainment purposes only. Professionals should be consulted as needed prior to undertaking any of the action endorsed herein.

This declaration is deemed fair and valid by both the American Bar Association and the Committee of Publishers Association and is legally binding throughout the United States.

Furthermore, the transmission, duplication or reproduction of any of the following work including specific information will be considered an illegal act irrespective of if it is done electronically or in print. This extends to creating a secondary or tertiary copy of the work or a recorded copy and is only allowed with express written consent from the Publisher. All additional rights reserved.

The information in the following pages is broadly considered to be a truthful and accurate account of facts, and as such any inattention, use or misuse of the information in question by the reader will render any resulting actions solely under their purview. There are no scenarios in which the publisher or the original author of this work can be in any fashion deemed liable for any hardship or damages that may befall them after undertaking information described herein.

Additionally, the information in the following pages is intended only for informational purposes and should thus be thought of as universal. As befitting its nature, it is presented without assurance regarding its prolonged validity or interim quality. Trademarks that are mentioned are done without written consent and can in no way be considered an endorsement from the trademark holder.

Introduction

Congratulations on downloading this eBook and thank you for doing so.

This eBook is written with the intention of giving the reader an insight into the world of Cryptocurrencies (digital money) and how to profit from them.

When you think of trading or investing, you probably think of stocks and bonds. You might also think of commodities and currencies. In any case, walking around a shared store director's office and specifying Bitcoins would most likely get you an odd look, expecting he or she is not a devoted user of TechCrunch.

Cryptographic money is a type of advanced cash that is intended to be secure, and much of the time, mysterious. It is money related with the web that utilizations cryptography, the way

Cryptocurrencies

toward changing over neat data into a practically uncrackable code, to track buys and exchanges.

Cryptography was developed during the war in the 30's to secure their correspondence. It has advanced in the computerized world with components of numerical hypothesis and software engineering to wind up plainly an approach to secure interchanges, data, and cash on the web.

Bitcoin was introduced in 2009 and is computerized money in which encryption methods are utilized to direct the era of units of cash and confirm the exchange of assets, working autonomously of a national bank.

There are many books on this subject on the market, but this one may give you some heads up on what it takes to be in an elite group of Cryptocurrency investors while some tips and secrets to making a profitable business.

Thanks again for choosing this book! Every effort was made to ensure it is as full of useful information as possible. Please enjoy!

Chapter 1:

Cryptocurrencies

How do they work? A digital currency keeps running on a blockchain, which is a common record or report copied a few times over a system of PCs. The refreshed report is dispersed and made accessible to all holders of the cryptographic money.

Each and every exchange made and responsibility for single digital money available for use is recorded in the blockchain.

The blockchain is controlled by "miners," who utilize effective PCs that count the exchanges. Their capacity is to refresh each time an exchange is made and furthermore guarantee the genuineness of data, in this way determining every exchange is secure and is prepared legitimately and securely.

Cryptocurrencies

As installment for their administrations, diggers are paid physically printed digital currency as charges by sellers or traders of every exchange.

The estimation of the cryptographic money varies in light of interest and supply, despite the fact that there is no settled an incentive for it. Purchasers and merchants concur on a value, which is reasonable and depends on the estimation of the digital money exchanging somewhere else.

Since there is no delegate like bank engaged in the exchange, as it is a distributed exchange, the exchange expense that is related to charge cards is wiped out. The character of the purchaser and vendor are not uncovered. Be that as it may, every last exchange is made open to every one of the general population in the blockchain organize. One can obtain a cryptographic money through trades discovered on the web or exchange it for customary monetary forms.

Cryptocurrencies are exchanged through their own payment network. The Bitcoin (one of now many of these currencies), can be stored in a virtual wallet which a decentralized, peer-to-peer currency that relies on cryptography to facilitate currency generation and transactions. To

Chapter 1: Cryptocurrencies

prevent extra costs, computers called, "miners," receive transaction free Bitcoins for running a proof-of-work system.

Some authentic merchants have taken to Bitcoin, enabling clients to buy genuine items and services with the advanced money. You cannot purchase your ordinary goods with Bitcoins yet, but you can donate or give to a worthy charity, purchase Reddit Gold, buy common household items, gift cards, video games, some restaurants or coffee shops, and you can use to travel, and other items not listed. While some regular merchants have investigated tolerating Bitcoins as well, the vast majority of the interest for the cash has been energized by examiners, as opposed to early adopters. Instead of sending a message to an email address, you are sending money to a Bitcoin address.

If you want to pay for things with Bitcoin, you need a Bitcoin wallet like *Coinbase*. It's a simple website application that allows you to securely store your Bitcoins and then sell them. Coinbase is one of the major Bitcoin trades, which enables you to purchase and offer Bitcoins however you see fit. You join, store certifiable cash, and trade the money with generally low expenses. You can

Cryptocurrencies

pay for things out of your digital wallet or make a payment using QR codes.

Digital forms of money have been the most energizing monetary point of 2017 for some speculators and in light of current circumstances. Bitcoin bounced in value, achieving highs of more than $3,000 prior this year 2017. Ethereum and Ripple, the second-and third-biggest computerized monetary standards by showcase capitalization share, separately, picked up to 30 or even 40 times their value focuses toward the begin of the year.

Mining operations are taking off, driving illustrations cards supplies to nil and cost out of this world also. So by what means would investors – those that are new to digital money amusement – be able to profit on this energizing new region of speculation?

Bitcoin's History

As indicated by Bitstamp, starting today the market capitalization is over $12 billion with more than 12 million Bitcoins in the framework. Until 2013, Bitcoins were exchanging for as little as $10 each. When 2013 began, Bitcoins appeared to ever-increment in esteem until April

Chapter 1: Cryptocurrencies

9 where they crested at well-finished $200. By April 16, 2013, Bitcoins had lost almost half their value.

Since April, Bitcoins had made an incredible rebound. Bitstamp demonstrates that the cost of a Bitcoin didn't top until November 2013. In any case, in this same month, Bitcoins surged up to well finished $1,000 a piece. At the present time, mid-2017, they have risen to almost $3,400 each. You can make all the predictions for the future, but no one knows what that will be for Bitcoin or for any digital currency. Could digital currencies develop into an everyday currency?

Bitcoin is no longer the top blockchain in the cryptocurrency market. But, there is increasing room for other players, including some very large technology companies that are just getting into Cryptocurrency and realizing the value here. Some organizations are surpassing Bitcoin so far in 2017, with Dash and Ethereum increasing 600% and 550% separately so far this year.

What is next for digital forms of money? Top investors expect that the market top will reach $300 billion by 2021. Diverse financial specialists are indicating different monetary forms and items as the following enormous thing, yet the idea that there will, to be sure, be a next huge thing by any stretch of the imagination, is by and large taken as guaranteed.

There are four ways to get coins:

1. Mining/forging rewards

These are coin rewards that are designed for incentive purposes for miners (forgers for creating new blocks in the blockchain). Depending on the price, difficulty, and capacity, this might be pretty much costly than basically buying coins from a provider that assumes praise card installments.

For instance, some companies only allow the top 100 agents to fashion new squares, along these lines barring other individuals from being eligible for producing rewards. It is cheaper to simply purchase coins with a credit card, Paypal or bank account.

2. Exchanging on a coin trade

Cryptographic money coin trades work pretty much like outside cash trades. The market price of a given coin is controlled by these exchanges. With coin trades, you require different digital forms of money to exchange.

Chapter 1: Cryptocurrencies

Some do not have credit card facilities. If you utilize a coin trade, guarantee that it is a reputable trade like Kraken.

3. Purchasing with a Mastercard is a good option, and one company to use for purchase is CEX.IO. They are reputable and sell Bitcoins. They charge a 2% expense on all buys and pass on the Visa preparing expenses to you the purchaser. You can also purchase them using your bank account, or Paypal.

4. Using a third-party conversion service that converts one cryptocurrency to another, for a small fee of course. Changer.com is a good service, and you can convert one type of cryptocurrency for another.

Storing established coins has become frictionless! For Bitcoin and Ether (another type of cryptocurrency), an application called Jaxx is great. It is available for both iOS and Android, and is secure, feature-rich, and updated regularly.

Chapter 2:

Thinking About Investing

Investors have proposed that some of these digital currencies are probably going to at last, flounder. In any case, the strength that wants the market when the items are more assorted along these lines is vital to the long wellbeing of digital currencies as a class. Likewise imperative to this stable environment is the expanding number of trades, wallet administrations, and other optional digital currency items. This implies digital money holders will never again be so intensely subordinate upon a solitary administration. The procedure of decentralization appears to likewise have been gainful to the fundamental hazard that individual digital currency holders keep up too.

What is next for digital forms of money? Top investors expect that the market top will reach

Cryptocurrencies

$300 billion by 2021. Diverse financial specialists are indicating different monetary forms and items as the following enormous thing, yet the idea that there will, to be sure, be a next huge thing by any stretch of the imagination, is by and large taken as guaranteed.

Pondering putting resources into virtual money that can be utilized to make buys, carefully sign contracts or hold and store of significant worth like gold, however, their costs may vary quickly and even crash without cautioning. That is the reason you should make sure you've done your research on the potential dangers, before purchasing.

There are unquestionably great motivations to consider when putting resources into digital forms of money. Most coins with a sizable base have gone up in an incentive as of late. The most widely understood digital currency, bitcoin, has been outperforming the estimation of gold, changing over many dollars into millions for early fortunate financial specialists. But it's not too late; this market is hot! What's more, not at all like gold, these coins can without much of a stretch, be effectively traded for gift cards or even spent specifically at real retailers like Overstock.com.

Chapter 2: Thinking About Investing

Of course, it is important to keep in mind that these currencies are unpredictable and can increase and decrease in value quickly, which has an impact on their costs. It's additionally difficult to foresee which digital currency will be the following enormous victor. Ether has rapidly picked up in fame as a cryptographic money with points of interest over bitcoin, because of highlights like the capacity to make brilliant contracts. Be that as it may, there are truly several virtual monetary forms available for use, including some others like PureVidz, Stress, and Allion.

Tech and money related goliaths that once expelled digital forms of money and blockchain are making overwhelming interests in the business. Blockchain new businesses are rounding up large amounts of cash in token deals. More open doors lie not too far off.

Yet, being in its earliest stages, the computerized coin and token industry is an exceptionally unpredictable space, laden with one of a kind complexities and dangers.

Luckily, various tasks and activities are developing to make new open doors and help examiners, fans, organizations and inquisitive

Cryptocurrencies

individuals discover their way into this quickly developing area while working around the entanglements and obstructions.

Digital forms of money of different kinds depend on mining to open units of cash for use in exchanges and trades. The mining procedure contrasts from cash to money however definitely includes entangled PC stages which unravel troublesome riddles, gaining tokens or money as a reward. Huge monetary forms, including Bitcoin, develop proficient mining units with significant equipment setups working all day and all night at these assignments. Presently, blockchain fans are making their own individual equipment stages with the end goal of mining lesser-known and rising monetary forms on the system.

Processing Power in Exchange for Currency

Other than Bitcoin, monetary standards and tokens are mined on the registering force that can be traded for units of money. As cryptographic forms of money start to grow they will achieve all the more comprehensively into the more extensive world, a bigger number of ordinary fans without generous PC programming

Chapter 2: Thinking About Investing

foundation is getting to be noticeably keen on getting engaged with the mining procedure.

Individual mining setups can be worked with normal PCs and portable PCs and for the motivations behind mining digital currencies. Machines require major graphics cards, and in fact, the sudden increase in mining centers is escalating the need for more powerful graphics cards.

Home systems need major setups. When mining for digital currencies, home computer equipment requires ample processing power. For this reason, many people venturing into this pastime are building separate platforms to mine for digital money in another area. This assures they are not interrupting their computer setup.

The growing interest in home mining is inspiring many companies to cash in as well. These computer platforms are not being built quickly enough for some companies." It's no surprise because some home enthusiasts claim to be making hundreds of dollars per month, and the systems do all of the work.

There are some online communities that have been formed to assist each other with tips on building these mining systems in their own home. When doing this, it circumvents the markup by companies selling pre-made platforms, but home systems also require additional maintenance and substantial expertise.

An at-home mining setup really does not guarantee instant or prosperity.

Many novice cryptocurrencies have yet to excel and may never see the rewards that have made with Bitcoins, especially recently reported. Although, fans of the cryptocurrency business see the rise in interest as a great sign that all forms of cryptocurrencies are gradually making their way into the public consciousness. Further, the more that independent mining businesses exist, the greater the amount of decentralization, and that is usually a founding principle for any of these currencies.

The blockchain is the primary mechanical advancement that Bitcoin presented. From a cash speculation point of view, a blockchain is a mutual open record of all exchanges that have ever been executed on a particular cryptographic money arrange.

Chapter 2: Thinking About Investing

It is a database of each exchange that has ever happened. The honesty and the sequential request of a blockchain are authorized with intense cryptographic calculations.

A blockchain comprises of many squares in which singular exchanges are put away. A block is essentially an information structure. Each time a piece is finished, another block is made. A one of a kind hash from the last finished piece is produced and put away in each new block. Each block is consequently ensured to come after the last piece sequentially and therefore, the last block's hash would somehow not be known.

This cryptographic design permits a blockchain to remain as evidence of all exchanges that have happened on any given system. A blockchain is kept up by a system of PCs (hubs). Every hub downloads a full duplicate of the blockchain. The hubs speak with each other and through differing procedures of dispersed system agreement; guarantee that the information in their particular blockchain is valid.

These are the fundamentals of blockchain technology. Obviously, each individual blockchain implementation has its own unique design, advantages, and disadvantages, but the

Cryptocurrencies

core principle remains the same. Blockchain innovation is the absolute most essential development since the approach of the Internet itself. It has the most potential for generally changing the route in which our general public sorts out itself and capacities. The decentralized idea of blockchain innovation can possibly redistribute control and reshape our political-economic landscape.

Blockchain technology provides scarcity of currency, near real-time financial transactions across the globe, very low transaction costs, anonymity, data security through cryptography, effective contracts, decentralized applications, distributed storage, and direct peer to peer transactions (which completely cuts financial and government out of the transactions).

Blockchain technology is still growing. Cryptocurrencies are seeing more and more sophisticated applications of technology with several new projects. No one knows what future will look like but it will almost certainly be distributed, and Venture investment companies are continuing to target new blockchain growth.

This is an overview of the different blockchain protocols for 2017. These cryptocurrencies will

Chapter 2: Thinking About Investing

monetarily change up and down quickly as their demand grows.

- Bitcoin
- ZCash
- Ethereum
- Ripple
- Hyperledger Fabric
- Corda
- Intel Sawtooth

The drivers of this demand can be attributed also to having a limited supply. Blockchains are somewhat difficult and the energy or electricity to secure can be a significant problem. The price of the Bitcoin keeps climbing rapidly which attributes to demand factors. There are also many scams out there to get your money by offering to secure currencies for you (invest) that you really have to be careful of. Digital currencies can take a dive quickly like the stock market, and you could be in for a huge loss. It just takes constant monitoring.

This is a huge opportunity but a risky one also. It is possible to make a lot of money or even a comfortable profit. This is a real learning curve. Make sure to do a lot of research before you leap.

Cryptocurrencies

There is a ton of research and a lot of advice from people who have actually seen their money substantially increase in a very short amount of time. There are literally hundreds of digital currencies now since their appearance in 2009. Each one is a little different in what they offer.

Efficiency and usage is an important factor in the price of cryptocurrencies. There wouldn't be much value of these currencies if you couldn't use them to purchase items or services except to save them for investment and that is not a bad idea.

Many people have hit the jackpot doing just that. The Bitcoin started out at 8 cents each. Today's price is well over $3,000 each. That's quite a profit in eight years time.

There are dozens of penny cryptocurrencies available now. You never know what they are going to do or how fast they may take off like Bitcoin did. There is a currency called AllSafe that went up in price over a staggering 15,000% in one single day. If you had invested $2,000 a few years ago, you would have over a million dollars in your pocket today.

Chapter 3:

16 Tips and Advice

The world of digital money is exploding in a huge way. It is reported that some people are getting rich very fast while climbing on board the cryptocurrency train. The train is starting to get very crowded, but there are a few cars still available.

This is an exciting concept market, and there's a lot of information to take in. While this concept seems simple, you are working on code and algorithms. To be one of the wealthy Engineers of this extraordinary venture, just be aware it is possible to become rich, it does not happen overnight, it takes time and a considerable amount of money to start and knowledge of all aspects of this opportunity.

Share your exact cryptocurrency portfolio with subscribers and provide weekly and monthly updates on the markets. Closely monitor news about cryptographic money, investigate many starting coin offerings and present chances to endorsers as they emerge. We've influenced a fortune in cryptographic forms of money over the previous years, and a few endorsers of have shared stories, including early retirement, because of becoming tied up with digital forms of money early.

The sky is really the limit for some of these digital currencies, and while the first digital currency was introduced in 2009 for approximately $2, it has made quite a few people very wealthy in less than ten years. "Ether" now, is the second most valuable blockchain by market statistics.

1. The first tip is when you have your account opened up, invest a small amount in this "Ether" smart plan as it is gaining in value as this book is being written. In 2015, Ether was available for $11 and this year it has already risen at least 300%.

2. Ignore Biased Sources. These are the place pump and dump plans, and different deceitful conduct occurs progressively. Many individuals who post

Chapter 3: 16 Tips and Advice

on sites that take into account crypto dealers are angling for suckers, posting deception and gossipy tidbits and seeking financial specialists and they will fall after it. Try not to play into their hands; look for counsel through trusted and fair-minded sources, and settle on your contributing choices likewise.

3. Invest Within Your Means. Try not to sink your life reserve funds or your child's school scores into computerized cash. This is valid for any venture, obviously, yet it bears rehashing: contribute just what you can sensibly stand to lose. You know the familiar axiom, "Plan for the most exceedingly terrible, yet seek after the best?" That applies here. With insightful speculation arranging, you'll do well, however, be set up in the event that you do not.

4. Set Achievable Goals. We feel compelled to underscore this as much as possible: Digital cash is not a get rich speedy plan. We assume you can shoot for the moon in case you're a tycoon, yet for whatever is left of us, this exhortation stands: Set a practical arrangement of profit for your

speculation, regardless of whether it's 5%, 10%, 15% or more. Furthermore, stick to it! It's a youthful and extremely vigorous market, and it can be disordered; do not blow up, and adhere to your long haul objectives.

5. Do not Panic. Set aside the opportunity to sit back, inquire about the most well-known organizations in the business and concentrate on what's happening in the market. Do not settle on the spot choices.

6. Do not Rely on Guesswork. As we stated, elective money markets can be insane here and there and are frequently capricious. Regardless of how brilliant a financial specialist you are, do not volunteer your vision of what the market's going to do next. Indeed, even the individuals who good with hunches (the brilliant ones), will get their work done before making a move. Take after patterns, read tips and news and watch recordings to respond in like manner.

7. Learn from Your Mistakes. Let's be realistic: Any market can resemble rolling the dice. Regardless of how great a

financial specialist you are, there's going to come a period when you get singed. Acquit the buzzword, however when that happens, lift yourself up, clean yourself off, and get back on the trail. The main unfortunate errors are those from which we do not get the hang of anything.

8. Chart Your Course. Study the patterns of the market over the long run, and figure out how to peruse and translate diagrams, (those offered at Bitcoin Wisdom). Definitely, track your interest progressively; however, do not settle on automatic choices in view of progressively self-insightful changes. Regardless of where you have your cash contributed, to purchase and offer given statistical information, is so important.

9. Love Thy Crypto. The universe of high funds and Wall Street can seem dry and ordinary to a ton of us; there does not appear to be a great deal of energy included. We genuinely trust that it shouldn't be the situation with computerized money. Indeed, do not put resources into the expectations this is every one of the get-rich-fast plans;

rather, do it since you absolutely accept the ideas and the standards behind digital currency.

10. Educate Yourself. If you learn and apply that knowledge, the better you'll do; that goes for computerized cash contributing as much as it does building an arrangement of bookshelves. Coin pursuit is committed to learning about the universe of digital money going so far as making a Crypto Social Network, such as "Slicefeeds," to help manage cryptocurrencies. The assets are there for you in the event that you reliably exchange ineffectively, and are unwilling to utilize those assets to your advantage.

11. Have Fun. Do not simply make your venture and sit and gaze at graphs throughout the day. Associate with your close financial specialists and offer your contemplations and encounters. Put some enthusiasm and fun into your advanced money encounter, and everybody wins. Life's far too short to simply kick back and worry; make your venture an improving and agreeable part of yours, all while making millions!

Chapter 3: 16 Tips and Advice

12. Buying and Holding Bitcoins - If you want to start earning bitcoins, you first need to obtain a bitcoin wallet, which is used to send, receive and store your bitcoins. You can obtain one from an online based service such as "Coinbase" or "Blockchain" These are two of the most used bitcoin wallets and come with an online and a mobile version. Having said that, the safest way to store your cryptocurrencies and hold it for future would be to set up an office wallet.

13. Day-Trading is the same as trading in the stock market, but instead of trading shares, you will be trading bitcoins. Purchase these Bitcoins when the cost is low; then sell them at a much higher price. The price you sell them for should be at a high profit. Of course, this will make it necessary for you to follow bitcoin news closely and regularly. If you are willing to spend the amount of time it takes to earn a profitable return with cryptocurrencies, then day-trading could be for you. There's a lot of profit to be made. If you can read charts or anticipate price movements, you can make money.

Cryptocurrencies

14. Earn Bitcoins from interest payments - On the off chance that you as of now have some Bitcoins, set your Bitcoins to work for you. Gain Bitcoins through intrigue installments by loaning them out. Loan straightforwardly to somebody you know. This enables you to evaluate actually, regardless of whether you see the borrower as dependable. At that point, you two just need to concede to the terms like length and financing cost and off you go. The downside is, in any case, that you most likely will not have excessively numerous associates who coordinate your sum, length and loan cost necessities. Be that as it may, it's a pleasant approach to gain Bitcoins.

15. Distribution Bitcoin loaning sites with postings from different borrowers are another choice. This site is such a shared loaning site. Borrowers distribute financing solicitations, and you can add to their credit. You can finance little bits of many credits and in this manner expand default chance. Bitcoin credits for the most part work an indistinguishable route from fiat money advances. The borrower gets a specific measure of cash over a

Chapter 3: 16 Tips and Advice

predefined time and reimburses the cash with premium. When you loan Bitcoins, there are a couple of things you need to know; the website should be reliable, and the borrower should be dependable. At the point when the website surveys the financial soundness of their candidates, the data given regarding borrowers can be more valid.

16. Earn bitcoins by "mining" which is the procedure by which new Bitcoins are created. When you perform mining, your PC adds new Bitcoin exchanges to the blockchain (an open record where all Bitcoin exchanges are kept) and scans for new blocks. A block is a document that contains the latest recorded exchanges. Then, when your PC locates another piece of information, you will receive a specific number of Bitcoins. As of now, a block contains BTC 25. This number changes all through time and decreases by the factor 0.5 at regular intervals. To earn Bitcoins when mining, be aware that it is a costly and time-consuming process but can be well worth it monetarily as time goes on.

Cryptocurrencies

Simply buy as much as you can and hold on to them. Ignore the minor dips and climbs, slowly build up your Bitcoin # as much as you can afford. In 10 to 15 years, your network in Bitcoin will be 20–50x more than now.

1. Take advantage of price moves

2. Consider "initial coin offerings.

3. Try mining and get ahead of Bitcoin and Ethereum

4. If you have a large amount, move some or all of your coins off the exchanges to minimize third-party risk.

Chapter 4:

On the Road to Make Millions

The two best options to make money with cryptocurrencies are either **mining or exchange**. By digging for Bitcoins, as long as the business sectors stay dynamic you can essentially profit to no end. However, the issue is, mining Bitcoins is such an extreme venue now despite all the trouble. Transforming your PC into an excavator will probably make it loud and warm up. It would require a big investment to try attempt to mine a single Bitcoin. That time and money could have been used on acquiring more PC power. Research other cryptocurrencies.

Notwithstanding, on the off chance that you approach some genuine processing influence and you do not need to pay the bills, you could profit here.

The more reasonable method for making a million with Bitcoins will be exchanging them through the most conspicuous trades, for example, Coinbase. In 2011, you could have purchased Bitcoins for $10. Essentially you ought to have purchased around 1,000 Bitcoins back when they were shoddy. This would have taken a toll you around $10,000 in 2011, making you a mogul today.

Making a million with Bitcoins today is likely to be conceivable, yet you will require some capital. Bitcoins can vary numerous rate focuses each day (on May 22, 2017, the cost hopped up 10%). Day exchanging Bitcoins will be unsafe, however where is there is instability there is an opportunity. Else, you have to adapt a more drawn out term strategy and close regardless of whether you figured Bitcoins would be effective or not. In the event that you think Bitcoins will be exchanged by remote trade merchants, advertising producers, and organizations one day, you might need to go long. Purchasing at this moment would be inconceivably dangerous; the value diagram is shouting "bubble," yet your purpose of passage depends upon you. Try not to

Chapter 4: On the Road to Make Millions

hope to see business to have quick development now, however.

Then again, in the event that you have a solid conviction in the defeat of the Bitcoin, you have to short the digital money in any capacity you can. This would be a greatly hazardous attempt still, however, if the Bitcoin showcase is really bound for disappointment, why not get rich when the air pocket pops? To short a Bitcoin, you will either need to get inventive or join a trade which enables you to do as such.

The Bitcoin has been attempted, demonstrated and is practically standard. It is still observed as a fabulous speculation opportunity. On the off chance that you resemble me, you missed the chance to get into Bitcoins while it was still generally shoddy. However, it may not be past the point where it is possible to get into Bitcoins from a venture viewpoint. Despite the fact that a solitary Bitcoin costs us more than $3,400 each, the cost might increase significantly as its mass reception proceeds. Remember that a Bitcoin can be partitioned to the eight decimal spots and that it will turn out to be exponentially more costly to mine as time proceeds.

Cryptocurrencies

It likewise has the snowball and organizer impact working to support its. There is no motivation behind why a solitary Bitcoin cannot end up noticeably justified regardless of a million dollars in principle, and numerous others trust it most likely will in the end.

Ethereum is a decentralized application platform that has its own Bitcoin equivalent cryptocurrency, while Bitcoin is a decentralized currency only, The Ether is sometimes referred to, as the world computer because it can execute any logical step of a computational function. This ability creates a myriad of application possibilities.

When Ethereum was conceptualized by Vitalik Buterin a few years ago, he was only twenty-two and reported to be brilliant, and the "Einstein of blockchain technology." Ethereum became the fourth highest crowd-funded project to date with backers investing over $18 million in the project back then. This blend of Ethereum's decentralized cryptographic engineering and Turing fulfillment could take into account already unheard of uses.

Ether is expected to increase much faster than Bitcoin's price did. This is because, although they

Chapter 4: On the Road to Make Millions

are still in their infancy, there are already operational decentralized applications that are controlled by Ethereum's (Ether) cryptocurrency.

Also, the idea of a "Smart contract" has been introduced by Ethereum, that is a contract inscribed in code that starts when placed in the Ethereum blockchain. An agreement can move around stores in view of specific conditions. This takes into consideration applications like decentralized escrow, rental contracts, and property deeds.

Share your exact cryptocurrency portfolio with subscribers and provide weekly and monthly updates on the markets. Keep track of all digital currency news; inquire about many starting coin offerings and present chances to endorsers as they emerge. We've influenced a fortune in digital forms of money over the previous year, and a few supporters of have shared stories, including early retirement, because of becoming tied up with cryptographic forms of money early.

A huge advantage to opt into this digital monetary technology is the fact that there is there is still a small percent of the world's population that understands the concept of

Cryptocurrencies

blockchain technology or even has any cryptocurrency. That will turn around when more people catch on to the different types of returns that are being created by investing in these digital currencies.

If you are new to investing in cryptocurrencies, it is extremely important to make sure that you find out about the dangers before you begin to work on sending/accepting small sums prior to contributing anything of significance. It absolutely would require additional investment and tolerance than just buying stocks in your money market fund, but the returns are well worth the effort.

The potential of blockchain technology and the investment returns of cryptocurrencies have been causing a lot of excitement. It is truly revolutionary technology that that is expected to have a significant effect on several multi-billion dollar industries. It is truly a once-in-a-lifetime wealth-making opportunity for those that invest early.

This is more than likely the only investment news covering both valuable metals and digital currencies with this measure of detail. They are both better than bank-issued fiat fragmentary

Chapter 4: On the Road to Make Millions

paper notes, and they both keep on increasing in their worth, while the dollar loses buying power.

With the meteoric rise in popularity of Ethereum, cryptocurrencies and blockchains are back in the news again. Graphics' card costs have taken off with the guarantee that the individuals who have the PCs and the know-how to do mining, can bring home tremendous payoffs in a Bitcoin-like dash wealth and grab as much as they can of this virtual money as possible. Be that as it may, how simple is it to make your fortune in digital currency? Also, is it worth your while to begin?

For the uninitiated, digging for monetary standards like Bitcoin and Ether implies committing an immense measure of PC preparation of energy to do bookkeeping entireties for the stages behind them, and confirming the accuracy of the general society blockchain records.

You're basically getting compensated for keeping the books for these stages, which we've clarified in more detail here, and the ascent of cryptographic forms of money like Bitcoin and others. This surge of qualified individuals has them entering the mining business in hopes of profiting! A dream come true!

One approach to profit from cryptocurrencies is through mining them. Without a doubt, mining digital money is a procedure which requires PC programming know-how and in addition sufficient power. However, for those in a position to have the capacity to set up mining stations, the work usually starts to pay for itself fairly rapidly.

Computers that are used to mine this digital currency run huge quantities of processing power and use powerful graphics cards to solve those complicated mathematical issues.

The reward for solving these problems is a small amount of a particular cryptocurrency. Mining cryptocurrency means getting rewarded for keeping the cryptocurrency platforms' books.

What's important to keep in mind about mining operations is that serious miners will have many rooms set up and full of incredibly powerful computing platforms. It will take a warehouse full of computers working around the clock to mine for cryptocurrencies, to be competitive enough and make a lot of money.

Chapter 4: On the Road to Make Millions

Playing the Exchanges - If you're interested in getting some of the most recent cryptocurrency tokens but do not want to take the time and resources to make a mining platform, your next best option is to purchase the tokens from an exchange. Although this will not be a fast access to the newer currencies as it would if you were mining for them but it would be a way to earn some money outside of mining.

Some investors have been extremely successful turning profits by buying and selling on exchanges due to their knowledge and expertise as savvy traders. They start out with a substantial asset pool picking their exchanges carefully. It cannot be stressed enough to do your research first, select your exchanges making sure they are reputable, and then secure them as soon as possible. Then keep track of currency prices you are watching.

Due to the currency prices being so volatile, if they are delayed by even slightly, it can mean the either a substantial transaction profit or a minimal profit. Use common sense and pay careful attention to the digital currency trends. You just need a little bit of luck!

Cryptocurrencies

Keeping the ledgers for cryptocoin requires the use of some free software tools and a dedicated pc platform. Several years and you could use a home pc and monitor digital currencies to make a few dollars. Now in 2017, you can literally waste a weekend and a month's worth of wages trying to build a pc with four graphics cards or more and not make much money!

Graphics processing units (GPUs) are now the mining processors preferred in most cases. The graphics cards used are marketed especially for miners because they are better performing in difficult time consuming and repetitive tasks, where CPUs are better at quickly switching between many tasks.

There are many ways to get rich through Bitcoin investment mining, or direct mining of bitcoin but would require super-computers to achieve them.

Another option would be "pool-mining" where you could get commissions of already established mining companies.

Carry Trade is buying and keeping the bitcoin in your wallet for at least 365 days. Trading bitcoins is where, with proper trading skills, you can rack

Chapter 4: On the Road to Make Millions

up large quantities of bitcoins, rather than just waiting for it to rise and fall and trade them. Joining MLM networking programs could help you rack up some coins too, but you have to do a lot of publicity.

Excitement about investing in Bitcoin and Emerging Cryptocurrencies has been generating considerable profits. Precious metals and cryptocurrencies are both philosophical/political similar and considered purchasing at the same time. A good idea would be to have silver bitcoins and gold, along with a top digital currency, in your portfolio. They are all very promising **commodities, and the returns** could be substantial.

Profit potential in cryptocurrencies is incredible. The price of a single Bitcoin was approximately $5 in 2012 and is over $3,400 today. It is incredible how much it has increased in just five years. Although, be aware that because *of this dramatic rise in profits does not necessarily mean it will still climb. There are many more* cryptocurrencies being introduced into the forefront that could perform well or even better than Bitcoin or Ether have. Bitcoin now has a market capitalization of almost $20 billion.

Cryptocurrencies

While the majority of the consideration is on Bitcoin, 2017 is most likely the time of the altcoin, which just stands for elective (to Bitcoin) advanced monetary forms/coins. There are such a large number of now that it is difficult to monitor them all. However, they are positioned by advertising capitalization, here. I have recorded the Top 12 cryptocurrencies underneath.

The #2 coin with a market top of $4.2 billion is Ethereum. It is up more than five times (400%) since the beginning of 2017, from under $10 to over $50 per coin. Ethereum's originator, Vitalik Buterin, brought keen contracts into the universe of digital money and there are many maturing ventures being based on the Ethereum stage.

Ethereum's innovation can disturb numerous high-esteem businesses, and would be worth adding this cryptographic money to your portfolio. Although, it is not just Bitcoin and Ethereum that have been creating monstrous additions for speculators; "Dash" began it digital currency emergence at around $10, then shot up to $115, *and* is as **of now exc**hanging at approximately $300 per coin.

Chapter 5:

Investors Beware

G etting rich from Bitcoin by investing is possible, but you must be careful about many kinds of scam and hype programs and be cautious "There's no 'best' or 'easiest' way to getting rich."

It would be terrible to find one day that a hacker made off with your machine that had at least $20,000 of your digital funds. Thank goodness Cryptocurrencies are decentralized. There's no person or Bank waiting for your deposits, and no centralized trusted an unknown entity that is making everyone's life miserable and frightening. Power has a great responsibility, and there's no one to call to have your money returned to you. You cannot take anyone to court, or have anyone refund your money. There is no transaction to record. You can only report

Cryptocurrencies

your computer stolen. Also, no one will reset your security information if you cannot remember it.

If you die while working, then you're dead; simple as that. If someone steals your Bitcoins; then your Bitcoins are gone. It's entirely up to you to keep your possessions safe. You need to be completely honest with yourself.

Are you sure you can tackle this? If you cannot, then it is better not to own any of them. If things seem to be going well, it does not mean that they cannot suddenly go wrong. Machines and hard drives crash, USB sticks will fail. Sometimes if you are very tired, you can accidentally click an attachment you shouldn't have and then notice you now have opened a virus.

The most important thing to remember is that you need a well-known antivirus program installed on your system(s). Maybe even have several. That way you can have them on all of your home or office equipment plus your smartphone. Have as many as you can, but the very best thing to have is off-site backup systems.

Chapter 5: Investors Beware

Take some good advice and back "everything" up in more than one place. That way if something happens, you will always have another copy.

People that have been in the tech world have survived for so long because of being religious about backups. If a backup goes down, you will spend all night making sure it comes back online, even though it was saved many times, you will just want to make sure **you have it before you can rest. The computers are not what matters, but what's saved on them that is extremely valuable and cannot be replaced if there is no backup.** If your laptop were to suddenly burst into flames, it wouldn't be a problem if you had that crucial information on a good outside backup system. Computers and software can be replaced but your data cannot. If it is gone, it is gone for good. It would be devastating.

Get yourself an external hard drive or two**, and** pick up a few USB sticks while you're at it. When backing up your digital wallet, you do not need a lot of hard drive space. 16GB is a good size. Never use just one backup hard drive or USB stick drive and think that is good enough. You will be sorely sorry.

Cryptocurrencies

Off-site backup is the most critical move you can make. It is the most import thing you can **do to secure your data. Backup** your computer internal drives and your digital currency portfolios and information on external drives and travel stick drives and put them in a fire-proof safe or safety deposit box. Banks can actually be good for something! You might even want to put several stick drives in there. Having a backup stick drive located your bedroom nightstand is not much good if there is a house fire, flood or burglary.

But, of course, if you're carrying one of the stick USB drives, there is a good likelihood it will become a missing critical item. These little stick drives can easily fall out of your pocket, or someone can take them.

That is why you might also consider backing up to an online cloud or member program like **Backblaze** which allows you to create your own encryption code, which is imperative. Never, ever trust someone else to manage your private keys for any reason even though Backblaze has their own encryption, it is better not to trust it fully. Only backup files you've *already encrypted* yourself.

Chapter 5: Investors Beware

Sensitive data should always be encrypted to be on the safe side. storing sensitive data, you'd better encrypt it. **Veracrypt is recommended.** Another popular encryption tool is TrueCrypt, which is a great software utility. Make several encrypted file containers for wallet backups and passwords. These files act like small **virtual hard drives**. Just make them a few GB and choose double or triple encryption.

Using virtual hard drives is great too because you can store anything; images, text files, spreadsheets, and videos. What is even better is that the whole file can easily be taken with you. All you need to do is copy the "cryptocurrency backup" file and copy it to a USB stick. Core wallets, like Bitcoin Core, which allows you to back up your wallet, by using wallet.dat that is a single file. It contains your own personal coded keys, password, and your wallet information. Dump your wallet.dat backup file to your crypto-backup folder. Make sure not to store your virtual wallets and passwords together. Any attack could be detrimental to your business and your lifc! Make sure you create **different unique passwords** for each container.

Connect them just when you need to use them and be sure to disconnect them right away after you finish. Do not leave them connected without you being there and do not connect them at the same time. It is irresponsible and a dangerous thing to do. You can also make a copy of the encryption program to take with you, right on your USB stick drive. That way you will not have to install the program on another computer, as it will be available to run and use right from the stick!

Do not trust a non-core organization. There's nothing scarier than seeing your money evaporate into thin air because of some errors created in the code. Stay with the core storage and be sure you set a very strong password; then and encrypt your wallet. However, for day-to-day usage, the core wallet's is slow, clunky and frustrating. It is so frustrating and time-consuming to start the sync processing and then have to wait 30 minutes or more when you are in a time crunch to get coins exchanged because prices have dropped considerably. Not to mention the entire blockchain is being downloaded.

Your first wallet choice should be **a core wallet.** Every project has them. This is especially important for cold storage. That's when it is a good idea to store coins offline if you want to buy

Chapter 5: Investors Beware

or store them. The simple reason is that if your coins are offline for a few months or even years, it is probable the format of the file will still be compatible with the updated last version of the core wallet. These core wallets are only designed to be stable and productive. It would be quite devastating if it was stored somewhere and forgotten and software changes and because it hasn't been updated all you have is a fancy multicoin wallet.

So for quick, day-to-day usage, Exodus can be use**d** for the beautiful, intuitive interface. It also has amazing anonymous **Shapeshift built in** exchange capabilities, that allows you to switch from one certain coin to a different one with having to sign for anything.

Jaxx is another good choice of wallets, both of these are multicoin wallets, but this wallet allows many different coins and is adding more in the future. It also has the added benefit of having a mobile wallet, while Exodus is desktop only at this point. That said, Jaxx is not as spontaneous. Both of these wallets are part of the **Electrum** system of decentralized servers and have been around since 2011. These wallets are which generated from a pre-created seed rather than a totally random starting point. That has advantages *and* disadvantages. A great advantage is that it includes a twelve-word passcode phrase which lets you create your wallet at any time and also you can do it from anywhere. You could literally delete the wallet, move somewhere, then download the software, plug in the passcode phrase and have all your money back. That's an amazing feature.

Exodus also has a security issue because it will only require your passcode when it starts up. If you attempt to send currency, it does not prompt you again. That's very bad, and it means if the software is left running, then anyone can come in and go up to your unlocked desk and steal your money. Jaxx at least requires a pin.

The Nano Ledger is a unique wallet. There isn't **anything like** it. These wallets are a little difficult to get, and the prices of cryptocurrencies have raised the demand for them. You can receive them in the mail. It usually takes about a month, and then you will want to test them right away. They come included with hardware encryption and an LED screen. At this point, I'm not convinced they're much better than a dedicated USB stick with Veracrypt. Also available is the **Trezor** wallet, which is another popular hardware choice.

Chapter 5: Investors Beware

Mobile wallets are useful for having a small amount of spending cash with you all the time. **You never want to carry a lot of cryptocurrency on your smartphone.** Carry just a very, *small amount* of cash. The sum of $20 to $100. The reason should be obvious. Also, secure your machines as soon as you can before they are hacked and your $10,000 worth of Ethereum. This would be devastating, to say the least.

Strongly consider using a separate bare metal Linux box or a virtual machine running Linux which is a minimal install of Red Hat Enterprise Linux or CentOS, or even a security focused-distro is your best bet. You need to lock it down.

It is kind of like walking into Whole Foods thinking that any random box of food you choose from the shelf will be healthy. Even though it says it's organic, it does not mean it's the right thing for you. By using Linux, you'll still have work to do.

And if you're insistent on staying with Windows, you have much more to do. You will need to run the program on a clean install, with a security program. Do not run the program under administrator. The admin users have much more power on Windows. The regular users will not be allowed to install software. They do not even have permission to change the time which means that malicious software will not be able to load on your machine if you have administrator privileges. So you need to specify yourself an administrator so you can install all your software.

So what security software do you need?

You cannot just take any freeware anti-virus and consider yourself protected. Anti-virus software requires constant updates and a dedicated team of professionals behind it to deliver those updates. Those teams cost money. The bad guys never sleep. You cannot afford to choose free here.

 Do not purchase an antivirus company that keeps track of and sells your data so they can profit, which is the way the free security programs pay for groups of virus-fighters. Even if their software is good at catching bad stuff, the trade-off is Big Brother living in your machine. That's a no go.

Chapter 5: Investors Beware

BitDefender or **Kaspersky** and **Malware Bytes Premium**. There is a free version of Malware Bytes, but it's not good quite good enough when it when your goal is to protect your precious Bitcoins and Ethereum. The free version is just an infection scanner that is too late after the machine has already been damaged.

There is a premium version that includes a real-time blacklist of suspect sites. If you attempt browsing a site that is blocked, the software will stop the connection, and you will not be able to open the infected page. You should not be browsing the web on your crypto VM, although you can do that on your everyday desktop computer.

The VM is used only for managing your money. That's it!

Eset includes a sandboxed browser used for banking. It is used to disable all plugins which are very useful for connecting to the exchanges when you want to do some trading.

Also, there are versions of Eset for Mac and Linux. Both of the systems can be infected with viruses and malware too. You will need to have them protected as well.

The last thing to talk about is if you are Windows, just know that it is constantly, secretly spying on you. It continues to send telematic data back to Microsoft. You will need to get **Spybot Anti-Beacon**, which is a free program that destroys spy engines.

Some system administrative techniques will secure a Windows machine. The best one is by removing your user permissions out of the registry keys which will allow Windows to start some of the programs.

Even if there is malware and it attempts to self-install, it will not start it up. Since you're not running the program as an administrator, it will be blocked from installation. Only when the machine is recognized and running in Admin mode, would it be allowed to auto install. So make sure your machine is not set up that way. If you need to install and set up genuine software, you can change it to Admin but do not forget to change back again when finished. It is a slight problem when are installing genuine software, but you can change permissions, then install it and change permission back to the

Chapter 5: Investors Beware

original settings. Finally, you need to uninstall unstable software from your machine immediately. There shouldn't be any web games installed and make sure there are no search bars or browser plugins.

Your friend is the" Two-Factor Authentication." You must enable this Authentication if **you are doing any trading on the exchan**ges. You will usually have to add software to your smartphone, like **Google Authenticator**, but some websites are slightly different.

When you have logged in to a major exchange site like Poloniex or Kraken, you will be prompted to enter a code from that you will get from your authenticator program. These codes will change every thirty seconds. Then, even if someone gets your password, it will not work after 30 seconds. Two-factor also protects your withdrawals which is critical. If you are moving funds from an exchange then into your wallet, it will ask you to again, enter a code.

If you happen to have neglected to get a two-factor someone can steal your password, they can enter it and will walk or run away with all of your money and get away with it, scott-free

Cryptocurrencies

! Without the two-factor, you're playing a dangerous game, and you will be the sorry one that loses. The simple fact is that there are countless examples of victims posting on forums stating that they had been hacked. They blame unknown secret scammers that might be an employee within the exchange or even some sophisticated foreign entity hacking team.

If you have not implemented two-factor authentication, you will have a real threat of someone being able to get your security information and stealing all of your funds. **Set up the two-factor** *before you add any funds into any exchange.*

People have many questions about exchanges. What amount currency should I leave in there? Most advice you will get will tell you never leave coins in the exchange, but actually, that does not make much sense because there isn't any reason to keep them there anyway. It is smarter to control your own keys.

Leave the funds there until you reach your price – if that happens at all because you will want to trade. You will not know when that time comes. It could be ten minutes or ten days. Eventually, you're going to have to trust the exchange or just

Chapter 5: Investors Beware

choose not to trade. Try to split your funds between multiple exchanges. Get on five or six of them. Then if one of them gets hit, they do not take you for everything you've got.

There is a tremendous amount of pain when getting hacked and losing your coins. No doubt about it. Still, security has gotten much stronger through the years. Every major exchange, knows they have to hire a lot of security engineers.

Conclusion

Thank you for making it through to the end of this book, and let's hope it was informative and able to provide you with all of the tools you need to achieve your goals whatever they may be.

If your money is in a bank, the bank owns your money. Anyone who's lived through a financial crisis learned this lesson the hard way. During the years of the Depression, banks nearly broke the economy. People worked all of their life so they could save money, and yet they watched it tumble. All banks did then was to keep that money as a hostage.

If you do not have the private keys to your money, you do not own your money. That's a lot to take in, but this is no game. **Take your digital money seriously.** To control your own private funds is unbelievably empowering, but also a big job and a tremendous amount of responsibility. It's a

Cryptocurrencies

huge undertaking that also takes a lot of very hard dedication and a lot of up-front funds if you want to get rich quick!

The road to being a Millionaire with Cryptocurrency is attainable. A lot of investors are jumping on the bandwagon, and it is getting more and more crowded.

Cryptocurrency is not owned by a Financial Institution or a Government. The money you invest is YOUR money. It just takes dedication and perseverance to keep it growing and safe.

Good Luck and I hope you are on your way to millions of dollars!

Finally, if you found this book useful in any way, a review on Amazon is always appreciated!

www.ingramcontent.com/pod-product-compliance
Lightning Source LLC
Chambersburg PA
CBHW050019230526
45470CB00003B/1036